A Collection of Poems
1955-1988

ROBERT NYE

A Collection of Poems

1955-1988

HAMISH HAMILTON

LONDON

HAMISH HAMILTON LTD
Published by the Penguin Group
27 Wrights Lane, London W8 5TZ, England
Viking Penguin Inc, 40 West 23rd Street, New York, New York 10010, U.S.A.
Penguin Books Australia Ltd, Ringwood, Victoria, Australia
Penguin Books Canada Ltd, 2801 John Street, Markham, Ontario, Canada L3R 1B4
Penguin Books (N.Z.) Ltd, 182–190 Wairau Road, Auckland 10, New Zealand

Penguin Books Ltd, Registered Offices: Harmondsworth, Middlesex, England

First published in Great Britain 1989 by
Hamish Hamilton Ltd

Copyright © 1989 by Robert Nye

1 3 5 7 9 10 8 6 4 2

British Library Cataloguing in Publication Data
CIP data for this book is available from the British Library

ISBN 0–241–12843–9

Typeset at The Spartan Press Ltd,
Lymington, Hants
Printed in Great Britain by
Butler and Tanner Ltd, Frome, Somerset

Contents

THE WHITE FAWN

My weird's a fallow fawn, wild in the forest.
From Avalon she came, the bright foam skipping;
I know her presence by a scent of apples.

All summer long to catch her many Robins
In common green chased fleetly after moonbeams.
They dine on dreams who follow in her hoof-prints.

White is her coat and sallow her complexion;
No horns spring from that head so gently dipping.
I saw her once, and can adore no other.

Now, with midwinter come, and all fools parted,
Fulfilled of love I run, unfellowed, longing,
If only to touch snow her rut has rusted.

EURYNOME

Forgive me, Lord, who do not beg your pardon
Because I serve the lady of the garden,
Our mother Eve, who coupled once in Eden
Under the tree of life with father Adam.
She is Eurynome, the moon, my madam,
And there is none as wise or true or fair
In the wide earth, nor in the upper air.

SO WHAT

So what if Orpheus' singing head
Dispraised Beatrice as it bled?
And Dante coming back from hell
Recalled Eurydice as well?
She who is queen of earth and air
Is richly named as she is rare.

LISTENERS

Listening silence in the glass
The listening rain against.
All in the silent house asleep,
The rain and the glass awake;
All night they listen for a noise
No one is there to make.

All in the silent house asleep,
The rain and the glass awake;
Listening silence in the glass
The listening rain against.
All night they listen for a noise
Their silence cannot break.

A SONG OF SIXPENCE

My thumbs prick upon consequence.
Moths brush the wafers of grass
And the stickleback feels his thimble
Underwater house tremble
Where their warfare was.
In the black stream is sixpence.

Into my purse I put sixpence,
Nor bite my little finger at the words
Ants whisper round the chambers
Of a tussock of those strangers
Unwelcome to our tryst in the dark woods.
My thumbs prick upon consequence.

To pay whoever comes with no pretence
I have picked up this silver sixpence.
My thumbs prick upon consequence.

KINGFISHER

His majesty the kingfisher bird often
Stands on the snow's wrist all night long,
Unbubbling at morning the film of fire,
The big chrysalis of his blue wings.

Kingfisher, fisherking, a melting music,
He falls, a sword-bright shadow, through the dusk,
A sapphire spark, a hole in heaven, head-
long Lucifer, wanderer in new winds.

Minnows and other mercies serve the king,
Shoot down the frosty stream like spindrift stars.
My cruel flame, my lambent royal watcher,
Flickers above them, quick in the tight air.

THE SEWAGE PIPE POOL

I'd walk out on this sewage pipe to see
The quick, rich, swarming secrets of the pool.
Fat shrimps like garnets glowed in it – red crabs
Clawed sideways through its slime – once a pipe-fish
Got stuck, snout-up, half-baked in gummy scum –
And there was always bladder-wrack to pop,
A cluster of black grapes from the sea-bed.
I'd stir the lot with my stick. I was ten,
A good boy, not unhappy to be there.
Girls making cheeses with their petticoats
Also beguiled me, but the pool was best
Because its mysteries were mine to know
And my stick altered it and made them plain
Or readable at least, each barnacle
And rag-worm, goby and smudged jelly-fish
Part of a plot I spun, though not my own.

RIPOSTE

Above all other nights that night be blessed
On which my grandam rose from her sweet rest
Woke by a nightingale whose passionate song
Rang in the moonlight, Keatsian and long.
My grandmother threw open wide her door
And listened for a minute, not much more;
Then, when sufficient nightingale she'd heard,
Cried out: *Right! Just you bugger off, you bird!*

CHILDHOOD INCIDENT

One summer day at noon in our family kitchen
In my twelfth year I watched my mother cooking
The Collected Poems of Elizabeth Barrett Browning.

This was, I must admit it, a dirty book.
I had picked it out from an even dirtier junk-stall
Down in the market, near the church that used the
                                        incense.

Mrs Browning, as I remember, cost me sixpence –
Which was all my pocket money, plus a penny
                                        borrowed,
But I forked out for her gladly on account of her
                                        famous love.

Alas as I took the book from the Pakistani stall-keeper,
Wiping the dirt of the years from it with my shirt
                                        sleeve,
This funeral came out of the church that used the
                                        incense . . .

Back home, my mother saw red at the sight of Mrs
                                        Browning
And when, in my stammering, I blurted out about the
                                        Pakistani
And then the purple coffin – well, it was just too much!

My mother took Elizabeth Barrett Browning in a pair
                                        of fire-tongs
And deposited her in the oven, turning the gas up high,
Remarking that this was the way to kill all known
                                        germs.

8

I feared then that what I would see would be the
                                        burning
Of Elizabeth Barrett Browning in our family kitchen;
But, praise to God, my mother knew her regulos.

I remember the venial smell of the baking
Of Elizabeth Barrett Browning in our family kitchen.
I can still see those pages that curled and cracked,

And the limp green leather cover that peeled away like
                                        lichen
From the body of the book, and the edges turning
                                        gold,
And the hot glue's hiss and bubble down the spine.

But most clearly I recall as if this was just yesterday
An odd but quite distinct and – yes – *poetic* scent
Which arose from the remains of Mrs Browning's
                                        Poems

When they came out baked and browned from my
                                        mother's oven
And lay steaming there on the table in the family
                                        kitchen.
It was, I swear to God, a whiff of incense.

GOING TO THE DOGS

Come Friday night my father's public vice
Was a greyhound track. He took me there twice.
Most of his life his own sad way he went,
So going to the dogs with me was different.

The electric hare, the eager racing hounds,
Tic tacs in their white gloves, fistfuls of pounds –
The magic of that place and its event!
Oh, to me going to the dogs was different.

To choose a trap my poor Dad bruised his wits
Perusing form, and when that failed had fits
Of asking me my fancies. What this meant
For us made going to the dogs quite different.

Once the choice dog in the pre-race parade
Excreted what looked like bad marmalade.
'A sign,' my father said, 'from heaven sent!
You do know going to the dogs is different?'

He'd urge his favourite home with passionate cries.
The keenest still brings tears into my eyes:
'Come on, my son!' It was an accident
Which our dear going to the dogs made different.

I can't remember what my old man won;
God knows he lost much more in the long run.
His coat was shabby and his hat was bent,
But going to the dogs I found him different.

I do recall my father shook my hand
When our dog came in first. Now understand:
Some of us gamble when our hearts are spent.
My going to the dogs is not so different.

REFLECTION

Foreigner in foreign country
Not my countryman,
Stranger to strange company
No stranger,
Logical interloper
I think you are benighted
By your own grief
Of fitting in too well.

REVENANT

If through that mirror's crack in not quite dusk
You see, or remember, the only ghost you know
Beyond your own ghost on the frost-worked pane –
Under a map of the Land of Cockaygne
A child asleep on his arms at a high desk,
Dreaming of puppets, poems, and sherbet powder –
Why not elect to love him, for he was
A boy who never learned to tell the time
And you're late coming home.

FISHING

At thirteen he went fishing for stars.
Either for lack of hooks or love of the strict twine
Which could be taught to shiver in the hand
He fished for them, saying he fished for crabs.

No bait gets glory. He used mussels.
After school he had searched the hard
And taken plenty when the tide was out;
Now each agape, its matter manifest,
His greed made fast with a half-Gordian knot
In a new context, and sent back to the dark
About its tacit business. He felt sure
Some star that lurked or smouldered in the net
Of stars below the surface could be caught.

Crab after crab came up, acknowledging
His wasteful magic and his innocence,
But still no star rose clinging to a shell.
Once, twice, he thought he had one, but
Only an unlucky starfish floundered, half-wound
In the sea-stained twine, mocking star-need.
Sick of ambition, tired of self-deceit,
He lost his sleight of hand, let all his gear
Ride with the tide, and sat and watched the moon.

Later he learned how not to fish too much –
Or, rather, how to fish for more than stars
With less than mussels or a singing line.
He fished for nothing. And he caught the sea.

THE CHERRY TREE

His answer to the cherry tree
She peoples with lack-lustre fruit:
'This was a pretext of the night,
The nightingale's unlucky perch
For renaissance of his pain,
A darker index of the moon,
The radicle from foot to star
Both feet go searching for.'

Such protestations only show
That he's self-haunted, full of froth;
Not so much Truth's secretary
As clerk and agent to a ghost.
She asks the cherry tree to turn
This butterfly into a moth,
To wash the cherries from his wings
And dry his wings along dry bark.

A MOTH

'See, there, her face behind us, on the pane
Than runs with night. She watches jealously
While I undress your shadow on the ceiling.
She comes and goes between us if we nap
Too near the grate, or walk before this lamp,
Sleep-walkers leading the blind colts of sleep
For them to fill the steps we make for them.'

'Put out the light. There is no one behind us –
Only a moth who wants to die too soon.
Or let her in, and welcome, for she'll find
Fire's not so hot nor flame so flattering when
You have no choice but burning, and that's hard.
Now, sleep, and no more dreams. I'll leave my best
Shoes, heels under, to ride away nightmare.'

SAINT JOAN

A thing in the form of a woman
By name of the Pucelle
Was burned by the soldiers at Rouen
After a proper trial.
She was a relapsed heretic
And excommunicate catholic,
Apostate, idolatress,
Divineress and sorceress;
A devil from Lorraine
Whence devils come
In the dress of women,
As everyone knows.

GARETH TO THE COURT

You ask why I drink in the gutter?
Not for reasons of love, nor self-hate.
Communion was never my poison;
All I want is my own liquor straight.
So, lady, I smell of the kitchen?
My adventures, brave sirs, mostly fail?
Kind friends, as you judge me, put this in:
I never got drunk on the grail.

ROUND TABLE MANNERS

In a muck sweat you quarrel with them all –
The knights of the Round Table, squab and tall,
Sat down to meat.

There is a glamour on the hall – plates come
And go just as the diners wish, though some
Refuse to eat.

They say you have come here to spoil their feast
Whose real offence is innocence. At least
You took no seat.

See now the chessmen playing, square to square,
This game that has no purpose but despair
Or twin defeat.

You are a pawn in Camelot's strange chess,
Fit only to be sacrificed, or less,
Your play complete.

Let them say this of you when you are dead:
Although he lost his heart he kept his head
And did not cheat.

OTHER TIMES

Midsummer's liquid evenings linger even
And melt the wind in autumn, when bonfires
Burn books and bones, and lend us foreign faces.
At such a heart's November I might wish
There was some way back through the calendar
Again to find you and to lose your love.

I might – but there's no eager winter weather
To my remembering. Our appetites
Were satisfied with spring, and cloyed by June.
If August brought us famine . . . Well, no matter.
It serves us right that when I'd think of you
My memory comes hankering back to autumn.

The gloam rains slowly; fireworks kick with green,
Attach all marigoldal to the hand.
A weasel dancing by the sallows calls
Windsor to mind, and when you went tip-toe
By the breathing statue of the Copper Horse
For bashful fear it would come down to us.

The roundabouts and swings wear canvas shrouds
In gardens our ghosts visit. A bat walks –
Hare-lip, shrill membrane, hooks – as it were you.
A bat's newfangled walk, as it were you.
Dear flackering bat, or ghost, my faithless head
Has not forgot you, though our haunts are gone.

And you have gone, though your autumnity
Remains to vex me in each hip and haw
Which early frosts have ripened to perfection.
'Do not remember me for I am here
At other times,' you said. At other times
I can remember but have loved enough.

THE RAIN UPON THE ROOF

Listen. It is the rain upon the roof
Telling of who you loved but not enough,
Whispering of what is otherwise elsewhere.

It would be sweet on such a night to die,
Kissing another's lips, touching darkly,
Hearing the soft rain falling everywhere.

Save that the rain has voices which complain
You never loved enough, you were unkind,
You ran away, you left your heart nowhere.

Come back! Come back! The rain's regret may cease
But I will love you till my dying breath
And after, if there's after anywhere.

A CHARM AGAINST AMNESIA

No name you know reminds you now
Of who you are or why you go
Alone about your trouble in the snow.

Forgetting whom you would forget
You have forgotten more than that
And lost your mind's distinctive alphabet.

So if you trace your footprints back
To where you started, will that track
Supply the sure identity you lack?

The character of snow is white.
You cannot find your own delight
From marks made on it by your appetite.

Do not despair. There is one name
Which being known will make it plain
That you and wasted snow are not the same.

Call up the faces you recall
And see if from among them all
One hurts your heart and makes even cold tears fall.

That half-loved other is your fate –
Her name can turn you from hell's gate
And bring you home again before too late.

AT THE WINDOW

The least disgust betrays the heart's persistence.
You kiss the cobweb on the windowpane;
I watch your breath shrink from it, a warm fleck
In freckled glass, and am your man again.

TO HECATE

Hecate, I saw the sallows
Burn for you at All Hallows;
In a whirlwind of white air
You came riding the Night Mare.

Know, Beldame, I loved you then
More than all your hallowed men;
But, a child, I did not know
Why you whipped your lovers so.

Now with willow in my hat,
Witch, I understand all that —
Yet still fall upon my knees
When your wind whips up the trees.

NO SECOND SIGHT

I have no gift of second sight, no art
To look into your eyes and watch my heart,
Nor truthfulness to burn, yet still I love
Feeding the fire I am a shadow of
With not-quite-lies learned in that school of night
Where I was taught to love you at first sight.

THE BROKEN SEA

His heart (swollen or wasted with sea-music) cries:
'The waves are heart-beats on the shore.
How slow they come! A broken heart dies slowly.
The Sea is not in love with me, or is she?
The Sea has not forsaken me, or has she?
How cold she is! And yet I love her wholly.'
So more or less and mostly more
His heart (swollen or wasted with sea-music) dies.

SHADOWS

Seek not to be her shadow for
When night comes shadows go
Into the darkness following
Her footfalls to and fro,
Bewildered by her wandering
In the bewildering snow.

Do you suppose your silences
Will warm her shadowy heart?
Or that by lying at her feet
You'll learn her truthful art?
You might as well adore the moon
Where shadows end, and start.

DEDICATIONS

Begrudged by the promising pencraft of my name –
On the flyleaves of books I thought were mine –
Dedicating each poem to you as if
It hoped its nine letters would be read
Into the classic authorship, and free-hearted
Of Love-until-our-names-are-both-forgotten
(In such shorthands as half-admired their
                              remembrance)
I could not yet refuse to sign myself
Or much regret you and your books are mine
For I loved the girl who read them for her virtue
And now you have my vices and my name.

STOAT

As I walked home a stoat ran round
About me with a womanish sound
On feet that barely touched the ground.

Her eyes so used to rat and hare
Fixed mine in a moon-blinded stare
Until I saw you everywhere:
Your dress that drift of smothering snow,
Your face her face, your step her slow
And rampant dancing,
In and out, on tiptoe prancing,
Until I felt the hot flesh stir
Between my legs, and not for her,
Nor yet for you, but standing still
On whited ground, against my will,
I felt my heart leap to my throat
And cry out for the dancing stoat.

THE LARK

The lark from his nest in a hoofprint springs
Up, up and up, trilling dew from his wings,
And busily rests, and sings, and sings.
I watch and listen, wondering why
His song's sad sweetness, a laughing sigh,
Reminds me only that I must die.

MOON FEVER

This is the scene to which I keep returning:
The moon is in her shroud, the sky is burning,
Under the streaming stars a heron stands
Like a sickle dipped in feathers; on the sands,
Beside where she is fishing, a silver eel
And speckled trout lie spread in a broken wheel.

I see the heron shiver from her trance
And rise upon the gleaming air askance.
I burn for her, yearning to follow after . . .
But am brought down to earth by your wise laughter
Who call this my moon fever, kissing me
On my hot eyes to stop the things I see.

AGAINST PIGTAILS

You plait and braid up your bright hair
All the small hours of a long night,
Each shining tress tight-drawn to your delight.

This pleasure, madam, I can't share.
Being no hair-brained sybarite
I'd really rather we put out the light.

Besides, our tongues have tied one knot
Which our sharp teeth cannot undo.
What need then, hair-worm, of another two?

I need the not plain but unknotted you.

IN PRAISE OF LIPSTICK

You lick your lipstick half the night
Yet have no need of this red paint
Whose lips are hot enough to burn a saint.

Sweet, such cosmetics serve you right
To put a new mouth on your face
So you can lie with me in my disgrace.

Lying apart, without delight
I praise your powder, salve, and scent,
While still suspicious what your kisses meant –

Lilies self-gilded look so innocent.

A BOWL OF WARM RAIN

Washing tears away in a bowl of warm rain,
Or with fistfuls of snow, or a melted moon,
Have you never wondered whether all your dreams
In the double bed are not worth the dreaming?
Whether your long labours of love in the dark
Are less than the kiss of well-grounded water?

Others there are that will greet you more sweetly
And touch you more deeply than this lustral rite
Which imprints no character, cleanses no sin,
Purifying only the surface of knowledge.
Yet you know nothing of love till you know it
May be washed away in a bowl of warm rain.

THE SAME SONG

You dream a song and I begin to sing it
In a false voice, and so the song is ruined
That was word-perfect in your head. In anger,
You tell me to be silent. 'Still, how strange
That you should sing the same strange song I'm
                                        dreaming.
Perhaps I hummed or drummed it? and you heard.'

No, music, I've no natural explanations.
You did not sing – but I have mocked your song
In broken accents, for my own amusement.
One day with a true voice I'd like to tell
How sometimes we catch breath and sing together
The same strange song, knowing we need no other.

FAMILIAR TERMS

You say I love you for your lies?
   But that's not true.
I love your absent-hearted eyes –
   And so do you.

You say you love me for my truth?
   But that's a lie.
You love my tongue because it's smooth –
   And so do I.

You say they love who lie this way?
   I don't agree.
They lie in love and waste away –
   And so do we.

AN END

Dear, if one day my empty heart,
Under your cheek, forgets to start
Its life-long argument with my head –
Do not rejoice that I am dead
And need a more laconic bed,
But say: 'At last he's found the art
To hold his tongue and lose his heart.'

CANDLES

We watch two candles melt together
In their last moments wondering whether
Hot wax and wicks are twisted of
Loathing or lust or even love.
Such burns illuminate the mind
But leave a tallow taste behind.
Grease-stained, smoke-fouled, the unquenched heart
Still keeps its shining place apart –
A glass that doubles each bright flame,
Making more light, though not the same
As this which smells of what it handles:
Our incandescence in the candles.

DARKER ENDS

Here's my hand turned to shadows on the wall –
Black horse, black talking fox, black crocodile –
Quick fingers beckoning darkness from white flame,
Until my son screams, 'No! chase them away!'

Why do I scare him? Afraid of my love
I'm cruelly comforted by his warm fear,
Seeing the night made perfect on the wall
In my handwriting, if illegible,
Still full of personal beasts, and terrible.

Abjure that art – it is no true delight
To lie and turn the dark to darker ends
Because my heart's dissatisfied and cold.
To tell the truth, when he is safe asleep,
I shut my eyes and let the darkness in.

NIGHT WATCH

Watching for my son to fall asleep, I fell asleep first
And woke in a dream to watch him sleep in this world
                (of all probable worlds worst)
Where he must wake in nightmare, not born free,
And nod with one eye open, on me.

Not that I would love him for heaven's sake or, worse,
Make him immortal with a curse.
Dreaming he slept I kept him safe from harm
Who was keeping me awake, and my heart warm.

Lullabies, my jackanapes, are out of date
But to remember them it is not too late:
Sing hushabye then, however much music it take,
However I wake watching for my son to wake.

SONG OF THE FOURTH MAGUS

On Christmas night in ivory air
I seize the old moon by the hair
And drag her through the virgin snow.

The dark is cold as calvary.
The naked stars against the black
Web of the sky crawl spiderly.

Sleep, child, while you can, by Mary.
Ride ass-back in your dreams, in glory.
Tomorrow will exact another story.

A BAT IN A BOX

The long cold cracked and I walked in the cracks
To pay the rent for the first time in weeks
And pick our post up from the farm on the top road.

That done – 'Has your son,' said the farmer's wife,
'Ever seen a bat in a box? I have one
You could take back to show him.'

And I imagined how a bat in a box
Would beat its bloodshot wings, and comb itself
With greedy claws, and eat up flies and beetles;

And how, when hanging by the wing-hooks, it
Would sleep, big ears tucked under, as if cloaked:
And how its tameness might in fact confound me.

I did not take it, back down through packed snow
To show my son.
                    Why did I not do so?

To tell you, I would have to undo winter,
Thaw my bare spirit, waste its bitterness,
Losing the long cold with some deeper drifts.

A bat,
          in a box.
                    Just think of it.

A LOAF OF BREAD

I went to the road for food, and found
Common surprise in a loaf of bread,
Holding my breath with the breath of it
And knowing that when I breathed again
It would indeed be morning and a loaf of bread
Clean in the carton there with other
Necessary purchases
Of a son unprodigalled, trying to play father.
I had not thought I could be so astonished.

Bread! I sat under the hedge
Out of a hungry wind, and the just-baked loaf
Was matter of fact as I sank my teeth
Into its crust and nibbled, then took
Swift bites out of its good and risen wholeness.

If I'd remembered I'd have sung for joy
Just to myself and the loaf in the commonplace
                                    morning –
Joy at dismissing for ever, or the time being,
Guilt at the boy I was for standing
Outside shop windows, sly nose squashed flat
Against the pane, dreaming on galleons and castles
Of cream and pastry, marshmallow, doughnut,
                                    shortbread,
Until I thought I'd faint for want of those
Unnecessary sweets which were all I wanted.

I didn't remember till now, and now's too late.
'The birds have been eating the bread again,' you say,
Cutting the bad part out.
                    Thus satisfied –
With bread and the perfect alibi – how could I sing?

AN EXCELLENT MATCH

I am your glass, and mirror everywhere
The fires you burn to see, or fear to be;
The man you wish you were, I am for you,
Reflecting who you are in what we do;
Yet I am yours too much, too perfectly –

For look, our likeness has an end, and there
Beyond the glass, deeper than your self-looking,
I rage, in blank suspicion, and half-mocking,

Completed by the knowledge I can share
Those images you give me, your reflections,
Though these shine otherwise, in false directions.

It makes no difference even when the glass
Grows dark with more than night, or streaked with
day
Larger than likely. Radiance and stain
Fall on you in a cold familiar way,
Fixed in a constancy I cannot pass.
The colour black is busy here, that's plain.

GONE OUT

Whenever you leave the house I write a poem –
To answer you or bring your questions home?
When you are here my words belong to you,
You take my breath, not as you used to do,
But for sufficient purposes of speech.
You hang upon my language like a leech.

Yet when you've gone an hour the poem fades
And I have little left but blots and shades
Of meaning, and I mean all that I say,
Which draws me out to stand and watch the way
Through the dim valley, hoping you'll come back
To give my words the simple truth they lack.

STORM

Hearing the crash of thunder out at sea
And the first dash of rain against the pane,
Watching the lightning's jagged tracery
And curtains that blow in then out again,
You lie awake in the crook of my arm
Complaining that you think I wish you harm
Even while crying that you love me still
And always have and always will
Who might as well love any other foe –
And do, for all I know.

GATHERING STICKS

Snow in the wind and pine-smoke blown back
Down the awkwardly patched-up chimney-stack
On her house that's at home by the wood.
Gathering sticks in the frosty dell
I stop to watch that smoke, I know well,
Which has come from the fire of her mood.

Sticks will be chopped and new water drawn
From the spring in the side of a winter dawn
By others, that's understood,
But will they turn back with cleaner hearts
Through snow and wind to where the smoke starts,
And with better fire in their blood?
Perhaps they'll just turn, as I turn now,
Not knowing why, not caring how,
With a love that does no one much good.

AN ABSENCE OF NETTLES

I like nettles, but I took
An old scythe for your sake
To clean the way where you would walk
And make it possible
For your foreshadowed flowers.

An evening I worked there,
And another, longer; gripping
The ancient handles with a clumsy craft,
Swinging the rusty blade about my knees,
Crouched to listen to it.

The keen heads of nettles
Lopped without pity
Were raked and carried up
To a black-hearted bonfire;
The shaven earth was ready.

I plucked out such roots
As the hands can find,
And cast away pebbles;
Weeding and watering
The revealed ground.

But now – no flowers have come
To fit your shadows;
The earth will not accept
The seeds you sow. And who can care for
An absence of nettles, an ungrowing place?

ANNIVERSARY

This is the wooden wedding –
Five years marred or married.
You came of your strength,
I went of my weakness,
To a time where one said, 'I love you' –
Meaning, 'I am lost. Find me!' –
And the other could not sleep in an empty bed.

Now we sleep too well together
And our separate hearts dream variously.
Such self-caressing dreams . . .
You have learned my weakness, and it suits you.
I have wasted your strength, and it chokes me.
And yet you speak of this
As an anniversary. And so it is.

We will celebrate our wooden wedding
With poems written by sentimental liars
Who found love easy, a comfortable sun
To shiver under in chill complaisance,
And not as it is – the difficult moon
Crying, 'Adore me! Adore me!' and then turning
Her naked back on mortal adoration
To go whoring after other moons, other devourers.

It is an occasion for happiness
And we are happy in our perfect ruin,
Being wooden both and hacking at each other
In the name of truth, though it be only fretwork.
Five years marred or married –
Time enough for regret perhaps
In the next five, in the happier returns,
When the heart has turned to tin.

MONSIEUR DISGUST

That worst withheld which is my best
Shakes out wet fledgelings from their nest
And gives the hand where they would cling –
Bewildered, slimy, wondering –
To greet Monsieur Disgust as guest.

THE GRASSHOPPER

Patience wears out stones: and poets too
Are worn out by a patience
For poetry, and for the unquiet poem.
But is the grasshopper impatient when
She drowns in autumn dew, a meagre fury?

THE ROTTER

He wished his bones might dream without his flesh –
A dead mistake. But then he was displeased
With death, and the whole idea of rotting
Appalled the rotter while he was still warm,
Making him crave a good quick skeleton
Cleaned in the sea by fishes, or a skull
As innocent as steel made blue by fire.
No doubt the shroud of sense disgusted him.

Was it to put off going to bed with worms
He went to bed with other skin and bones?
Using a little blood to bleed to life,
He wished his flesh might act without his mind –
A lovely need. But then he was dismayed
By love, and never much cared for touching.

CROWSON

He died at the proper time, on Christmas Day
As we sat down to dinner – an old man
With no friends and no vices, blindly mean
With the kind of love that goes with being clean,
His chief possessions a sour bar of soap,
A flannel which reeked of him, and a steel comb
He used to keep his dry grey hair in order
Over the face as hard and proud as a doorknob;
A sick old man, but acting out his illness,
A broken man, but whole and straight in cunning,
A man whom no one loved or liked or pitied,
Whom we had wished would die, for the work's sake.
And yet, I think, I did not wish him harm.

Well he was dead at last, on Christmas Day,
And spoiled our dinner. 'Just like him,' said Twitch,
'To go and die now, after seven months
Of not quite dying. Just like him to save
His death for the wrong time, when no one's ready.
Who wants to lay out a corpse on Christmas Day?
It would serve him right if we left him, eh?'
And I agreed (although I was dismayed
Not to feel much beyond an amateur's
Distaste for death) nodding in a paper crown,
Grinning at brother Twitch across a table
Set out with crackers, beer, cheap cigarettes.

Dinner completed and our bellies full,
Half-cut we went to Crowson's room.
He lay, the oxygen mask ridiculously sucked
Into his blue mouth, fish-eyes mocking us.
Beside the neat bed, on the locker,

His watch ticked fussily; his corpse
Scarcely disturbed the counterpane's perfection,
So thin he had become in these last days.
Twitch belched. 'We'd better get him over with.'

And then Twitch bullied
That sticky carcass, punched it here and there
About the bed, about the usual business:
A bag of bones shoved rudely in death's costume.
He mocked the stale flesh, fey in this last gesture –
'A Christmas present, darling' – tying a bow
On the penis, where a knot would have done,
Flirting with the shroud
As if it were the dress of some gay girl,
Taking revenge for all the dead one's age
And ugliness, knowing he would come
To this too soon – and, most of all,
For spoiling our Christmas dinner.

This is no elegy, for I did not love you,
Crowson, old man smelling of soap and tuberculosis;
And yet, be sure of this, I did not hate you
As queer Twitch did, who used you then so vilely.
Am I to blame for what he did to you?
The question in its asking answers 'Yes':
For where did Twitch begin and such fear end
As made me stand and watch without a word
Your death's deflowering by a twisted nurse?
To ask forgiveness were another insult –
I will ask nothing but that you forget
You ever knew me, as I would forget
The big day I was born, keeping in mind
The day you died. I am forgetting now
In hope I will remember you more clearly
And in your memory wish no harm more dearly.

ROUGH OLD JOKER

He can cut straight down oak, to shape it well,
Just the right point, to make each piece a stake
For a white fence to keep black cattle out;
Yet with each blow he gasps as if the blade
Bit through his bone, and he the rough old joker
Who needed shaping, straightening, made sharp
To drive, or be down-driven, in the earth.
And is there tree-love in the way his hands
Chase down hewn sides, stripping the spills clean off,
Holding the finished stake up to the sun?
Or hate, perhaps, of knowing how this stood
As he has not, long in a growing wood?
In love or out, he knows his work will stand
After he has a longer stake in land.

WYCH ELMS

Outside my window two young wyches
Toss their sweet wanton heads in the sun,
Then lean together whispering, undone
By the wind, my favourite bitches.

SHADOW ON A HILL

From where I stand on this small hill
In the moon's danger,
My shadow runs down land not mine
Like a tall stranger.

Sirrah, you have a turn of foot
And wit denied me.
I am the worse for company
You kept beside me.

A TROUT

Waiting for you, I sat and watched a trout
And found some warp of comfort in the thought
That I might catch or counterfeit his style
Of silence, to and fro, a subtle fool
In the dark places of the yielding stream,
But in that deeper water where you dream.

Forgive me that I have no gentleness
To be at home with you, nor business
To know you thoroughly, and only you.
With nothing done and nothing much to do
I wait to take you coldly by the hand,
Shaken with love I cannot understand.

NOT LOOKING

You notice I never look at you when I speak?
Perhaps you have seen in this something crooked –
A fear of meeting your eyes? You would be right
So to think, for my shame of your knowing is such
I'm frightened of your gaze clean through me
Proving my meaning little to you. Yet it is not just
                                            this.

I have a way of not looking, as you see,
Which is also part of a way of seeing.
If I do not return the long stare you offer
To search me with, and you might wish I'd learn,
It is because your presence is too sharp,
Your eyes too dear for my eyes, to be blunt.

I was never exactly frank, you know.
Besides, it's suitable to talk to smoky air
Knowing you near at hand, inhabiting
The corner of my eye, and half my heart.
If I looked straight at you I might say much;
Might even speak of love, which would not do.

ROPES

Watching the old man and the young man
Take ropes from round about the belly
Of the hay-waggon, you said,
'See how the old man coils and curls his rope
And brings it straight to hand,
While the young man leaves his ungathered.'
I knew that you looked down on what I'd wasted
But had not care enough to take it up
And make a neatness of it for your sake.

ONE OR TWO SWALLOWS

One or two swallows, eager to be gone,
Over their heads passed where they sat upon
A tall hay-waggon riding from the sun.

He said, 'In autumn soon these flocks of birds
Will pluck the sky of music. Such cold chords
Send shivers down the spine. You mark my words.'

She marked his words and found it time to stop.
She was a poet so she shut him up.
'They're just like tea leaves in an unwashed cup.'

THE CHRISTMAS WITNESS

I call midwinter back to hear you cry
O look at that, my dear! seeing some twig
By the frost's kiss or a soft touch of snow
Abruptly gifted with how bent a grace.
You were the Christmas witness all December
Once it came down to broken sticks and stalks
Surprised into a glory of themselves,
Making me heed and keep that festival
In which dead things achieve a kind of life
Just because frozen vapour blesses them.
Without such lessons in the art of solstice
I would see nothing much worth keeping here.

A SMALL MERCY

Down in the wood the boys walk wild
Hunting for badger and fox;
Afraid of the dark, fulfilling its curse,
They kill what the moon loves.
Poet, be grateful they do not run
Nor hammer yet at your door,
To drive your pen through your open eye
And follow the night to its source.

JOHN DONNE AND THE CANDLE

Do you remember a summer night
The sky deckle-edged with clouds
When you lay reading John Donne by a candle
On shadow-explicated pages?

I held a glass of water to the flame
To show you what a caught star might be like.
When I huffed out that little glory
There was a smell of mandrake.

NOVEMBER SUN

The sun so low
In the sky today
A squirrel leaps over it
Going to his drey.

ECHO

Standing outside the evening
I clap my hands together
To make the green woods answer
And the low hill send back meaning.

NARCISSUS

There sits the boy Narcissus, or some such,
  Kissing his outcast face, and crying for it.
Not that he need enjoy himself too much! –
  We know he is in love, and dying for it.

VISION AND REVISION

To spite the Furies
Some poets blow
Half their brains out.
How furiously
Those half wits then
Fool with their verses
To please the Furies.

SONG OF THE HALF-CRACKED ECHO

Loving you might be
A way of walking
On snow on sand
On sand on snow
Between the breaking sky
And the broken sea.

Loving you might be
A way of dancing
On fire on frost
On frost on fire
Between the dying air
And the deadly earth.

Loving you might be
A way to remember
All I must forget
Forego forget
Between the breaking sky
And the dying air.

Loving you might be
A way to forget
All I must remember
Redeem remember
Between the broken sea
And the deadly earth.

TRAVELLING TO MY SECOND MARRIAGE ON THE DAY OF THE FIRST MOONSHOT

We got into the carriage. It was hot.
An old woman sat there, her white hair
Stained at the temples as if by smoke.
Beside her the old man, her husband,
Talking of salmon, grayling, sea-trout, pike,
Their ruined waters.

A windscreen wiper on another engine
Flickered like an irritable, a mad eyelid.
The woman's mouth fell open. She complained.
Her husband said: 'I'd like
A one-way ticket to the moon.
Wouldn't mind that.'

'What for?' 'Plant roses.' '*Roses?*' 'Roses,
Yes. I'd be the first rose-grower on the moon.
Mozart, I'd call my rose. That's it.
A name for a new rose: Mozart.
That's what I'd call the first rose on the moon,
If I got there to grow it.'

Ten nine eight seven six five four three two one.
The old woman, remember her, and the old man:
Her black shoes tapping; his gold watch as he counted.
They'd been to a funeral. We were going to a wedding.
When the train started the wheels sang *Figaro*
And there was a smell of roses.

IN MORE'S HOTEL

In More's hotel we touched for the first time
The mother strings from which all music comes.
Then everything in that translated place
Sang with the change – our room-key turned to gold
And burned in the lock; the bedside Bible
Fell open at the Song of Solomon;
The sheets were soft yet smelt like new-baked bread
And our hearts beat in a sweet harmony.

That music we heard once in More's hotel
Was mortal, absolute, a simple theme
Which, being known, can never be forgot.
Instead of variations, I propose
We might go back to touch a second time
Erato's well-tuned strings, for a new song.

A BIT OF HONESTY

Love is the name they give out in Tasmania
To Traveller's Joy, which some call Virgin's Bower.
The thing itself is sweet, though not as mania
Would have us say, nor bitter in its flower
As those made mad by it sometimes protest.
It is as good a plant as all the rest –
No less, no more. In English parts, you see,
The name for this same thing is Honesty.
Here's honesty for you. Long may it live!
I'd give you love, if I had love to give.

WITHOUT PREJUDICE

To Spindle, Shears, and Rod,
Solicitors for God:
Dear madams, ref. the part
Enclosed herewith, my heart –
Please note this doesn't fit
The rest of the love kit
Supplied me by our father,
Your client, being rather
Too big to go with my head
Yet not big enough in bed.

CIRCE'S FAREWELL TO ULYSSES

Nothing can make you deaf, God knows, not moly
Nor bees-wax, certainly nothing holy
Can ever make you deaf to the half-pissed
Buzz of your own voice droning, atheist,
Busily bumbling on about your wanderings
And wounds and Troy and cooking-pots and kings
And bets and navigational aids and your sciatica
And how much things would cost back home in
                              Ithaca.
You bum – here, take your ticket to hell's halls.
Tiresias could use your story. You talk balls.
As for me, sunshine, I've had more than enough
Of it and you, so goodbye to all that stuff,
And farewell, Ulysses! Ulysses to hell!
Sweet Circe wishes you safe home as well,
Requesting never again to hear, for choice,
Of your Life and Works, or your influence on James
                              Joyce.

HENRY JAMES

Henry James, top hat in hand, important, boring,
Walks beautifully down the long corridor
Of the drowned house just off Dungeness
At the turn of the century. It is 3 p.m. probably.
It is without doubt October. The sun decants
Burgundy through high windows. The family
                              portraits
Are thirteen versions of the one face, walking
On the thick trembling stalk of Henry James.
It is a face which looks like the face of a goldfish
Fed full of breadcrumbs and philosophy, superbly
Reconciled to its bowl. The difference
Between Henry James and a goldfish, however,
Is that Henry James has nostrils. Those nostrils
                              observe
An exquisite scent of evil from the library.
Henry James goes beautifully on his way. His step
Is complicated. (He nurses an obscure hurt. It is this
Which kept him from active service in the sex war.)
Listen and you will hear the trickle of his digestive
                              juices –
Our author has lunched, as usual, well –
Above the sweetly unpleasant hum of his imagination.
His shoes make no squeak and he deposits no shadow
To simplify the carpet. Henry James
Turns a corner. Henry
James meets Henry
James. Top hat, etcetera. Henry James
Stops. Henry James stares. Henry James
Lifts a moral finger. 'You again!'
He sighs. 'How can you be so obvious?'
Henry James blushes and Henry James flees and Henry

James goes beautifully on his way, top hat
In hand, important, boring, he walks down
The long life-sentence of his own great prose.

READING ROBERT SOUTHEY TO MY DAUGHTER

Mr Robert Southey had the makings of a haberdasher
With a candy-striped shop in Bristol or Bath,
A secondhand carriage and a bow-legged mistress
With Jacobin leanings, but ambition and his aunt
Drove him to verse –
For which grand vice
He had no gift, only
A self-consuming facility.

Mr Robert Southey had the honour
Of wearing the Coleridges as his albatross.
Bad Lord Byron made his name rhyme with mouthy
And dignified him with fire also
In his Vision of Judgment.

At worst Southey R was a wire-pulling turncoat
Using little epics as tickets of admission
To the higher reaches of what he thought society.
At best this esquire was a man who was better
Than anything he wrote. Coleridge said
His library was his wife.

O sweet O prolific O mediocre R
O ramblingly gallant and unimportant S –
I remember how after the penultimate breakdown
Worn out with hacking you trotted up and down
Just stroking the spines
Of your seventeen thousand leather-bound
                                concubines.

Mr Southey, man of letters, you worthy laureate
With such a thirst for righteous justice,
You more than once saw Shelley plain
And didn't care for it.
'what a dreadful thought of his wife's fate,'
You said, Sir, 'what a dreadful thought
Must have come upon him when he saw himself
About to perish by water!'
So much for fishy Bysshe.

O Robert O Southey, if poor Percy Shelley
Screamed like a peacock, you clucked like a hen.
You had a good heart but you geared it to royalties
And took too much care it was never lost or broken.
Yet tonight, Robert Southey, I thank you by name
For the measure of a story you took and made better:
Not too fast, not too slow, not too hot, not too cold,
Not too hard, not too soft, not too long, not too short,
But just right for my Goldilocks –
Too young to say thank you
Herself, but who loves you
For loving just-rightness;
Bob of the Bears,
Our Southey friend.

HONG KONG STORY

I

Robespierre is coming to the conclusion
The late Mr Sing Sing is turning into an agnostic.
The back of the Chinaman's skull is a cinema
Where slatternly skirts trail in the mud
While he waits out of sight for an ankle to show.
A lock of glossy black hair hangs over his face,
Ink on ochre, like a magpie's wing. He weeps too
                                  much.
He confesses to so many crimes that the Police
                                Commissioner
Is amused, then embarrassed, finally quite jealous.

II

Mr Sing Sing is a grotesque even by Hong Kong
                                  standards.
On the day of the murder he can't do his own hair.
The comb snaps. He trips over the encyclopedia
That serves him for a carpet. He lands on his head
By the door. It is not really a door. It is more
Of a ladder. He goes down it now for a lager.
Once in the saloon bar he delivers a rapid oration.
All he wants is employment as an artilleryman.
He picks up a sashweight. His hand is podgy.

III

Mr Sing Sing chants and the others join in.
He is inventing incidents in crusades.
He talks loudly, more and more sober. Some day
He'll cut it off. Yes he will.
He's killed all his prisoners.
(They seated themselves round the table in the death
room.)
The republic is an elected nonsense,
Ignorance multiplied by rice.
A scarlet carriage means a violent death.

IV

General Romoza considers his maps. Roads, red roads,
Leading nowhere. There is a fire on the ground.
He runs from the sea to the hole and back again.
He elects to take the coast road. That makes sense.
There is no sky, only a murky collection
Of curt clouds. His skill returns. He clenches
His eyes. The stars are no more than a bouquet of ashes
In his sight. The small stones sing in the sand.
The moon of course is repeating herself on the night.

V

General Romoza arrives at the noble mansion.
Italian Gothic, it boasts a porte cochère,
A pinnacled tower, bold gables, embattled bays.
It is approached by a long dull drive
Under a snobbish avenue of beech trees.
Its innocence is preserved by a stone lodge
With an archway entrance also. Chinese lanterns
Swing with deliberation from mast and balcony.
The General brings the column to a halt.

VI

War, declares Robespierre, is not what we came for.
See a little lonesome stray snowflake come down
Through the air, he adds, it falls and melts and is no
                                                          more.
Now see others come along in that soft gossiping way
                                                          together,
And as they drivel on you can guess they've evidently
Got something on their minds. O yes, say
                              Robespierre,
What they're thinking of is the rest of the bloody
                                             regiment
Massing up there in the clouds for an organized attack
That will make a drift thirty feet deep and stop our
                                                          tanks.

VII

Robespierre's men shift their feet in a vallum of leaves.
They have heard all this before and never been
                              impressed by it.
Robespierre approaches the Italian Gothic door.
Robespierre sits staring at the bedraggled skeleton.
(It is an inch or two shorter than his doubts.)
Robespierre's spirits rise. A pistol – certainly,
That appeals to the imagination. Robespierre strips.
He is on his way to becoming a logical sheep.
His body will be trapped in a wee black book.

VIII

Mr Sing Sing, flanked by guards, follows the Police
                                        Commissioner
Into the dusk of the church. The organ sounds.
(It is that sprightly 9/16 canon in the 8ve
Used for light relief in *Die Kunst der Fuge*.)
Mr Sing Sing tears at his magpie hair.
The worst of the General's men are sprawled on the
                                        flagstones,
Polishing their rifles. Robespierre pirouettes.
He salutes briefly. Are you aware, says the Chinaman,
That your stomach acids could burn a hole in the
                                        carpet?

IX

Mr Sing Sing's togs are even more ostentatious
Than his criminal convictions. He wears a hussar's
                                        jacket –
High-buttoned, bottle-green, with appalling
Epaulettes – a pair of white cotton trousers
And brown riding boots of soft Hungarian leather.
The flickering of a thousand candles illumines
The Croix de Guerre unjustly on his chest.
Robespierre has sausage curls and employs a
                                        professional
To pick flowers for his wife. You're a long time dead,
                                        he explains.

X

Sometimes I think I would like to live in Hong Kong
With Robespierre and General Romoza and Mr Sing
                                                Sing
On that island of sweet lagoons and thieves and yams
Floating off the south-west coast of China
Opposite the province of Kwang-tung, in the Si-kiang
                                                estuary.
They say its hills are serpentine, its animals few –
Comprising a land tortoise, the armadillo, a species of
                                                boa.
The public works suffer from the ravages of white
                                                ants.
It would be nice to sit there and eat pumpkin.

MY UNCLE

My uncle's hands were the colour of tobacco.
He sat and he listened to the river rattle.
He dreamt of logic.

My uncle's eyes were the colour of cider.
He sat and he listened to the rain coming on.
He dreamt of Dunkirk.

My uncle's hair was the colour of Bibles.
He sat and he listened to the Tilley lamp's hiss.
He dreamt of luck.

My uncle's face was the colour of allotments.
He sat and he listened to the tick of the clock.
He dreamt of forgiveness.

Now my uncle is dead and his bones are in the ground
And I sit and I listen to the river rattle
And I sit and I listen to the rain coming on
And the Tilley lamp's hiss and the tick of the clock
And my aunt making cakes in the kitchen.

IN MEMORIAM JOHN COWPER POWYS
1872-1963

Knowing the horror of the house
More intimately than its mere ghosts,
You practised to unstitch
The mirror from its silver
And write down your name without wondering who.
O Prospero, no elegy for you.
You have been sent to Naples, that is all,
And this bare island is the barer for it.

INTERVIEW

What's it like, though, being you?
The old dog growls and bristles. This is his favourite
                                                question.
Answers win prizes. Nothing interests him more.
Inspired by the pursuit of his own tail
He has written his poems to find out what he smells
                                                like,
And now here's another dog, a dog-fancying
                                        thoroughbred,
Just down from Oxford, trained to the minute,
On heat and eager to do some of his sniffing
For him, and to declare the crap remarkable.
Woof woof, the old dog says, *bow wow*.
I'll show you where I buried my gift!

FIVE DREAMS

I

I dreamt a dream, what can it mean?
I dreamt I went to a playhouse
Where my life was the play.

II

I dreamt a dream, what can it mean?
I dreamt I wore a crown of thorns,
Crucified on the oak.

III

I dreamt a dream, what can it mean?
I dreamt I crossed a rainbow bridge
But fell into the pit.

IV

I dreamt a dream, what can it mean?
I dreamt I wandered in green fields
Where sheep grazed and birds sang.

V

I dreamt a dream, what can it mean?
I dreamt I was a dry white bone
Which Love used as her flute.

ALL HALLOWS

Once as a child I saw the willows
Across the river at All Hallows,
Each one distinct although six miles away.
What brought them close and brings them now again
Sharp to the mind's eye like an icon of it?
An orthodox theology of tears.

PROLOGUE TO A MASK

I am said to be made in the image of a mystery
Which may never be effaced however marred.
The likeness of God lies in the correspondence of the
                                               will.
Adam ate of the tree of the knowledge of good and
                                               evil.

It is not known whether that fruit was sweet or bitter,
Nor if without it the mind would have had a better
                                               taste.
You may suppose your own death to be a mistake
At least until you have been mistaken by it.

Meanwhile we will have sin to be going on with –
Which consists of so many little sips of the grave,
Original and actual: the sin of birth
And the seven sins of contradiction to eternal grace.

Glory be to the Father and to the Son and to the Holy
Ghost.
We can't change human nature but God may
By means of a specific antidote
Which is called Christ and tastes like bread and wine.

POISON

I know a poison sweet and quick
As Cupid's dart;
One drop of it can be enough
To stop the heart.

Not nightshade, monkshood, opium,
Nor salts of lead,
Can do what this white potion does
Inside the head.

Nothing is proof against its power;
We die too soon,
My love, but there's no antidote
Against the moon.

THE LIFE OF BYRON

Byron beside Augusta found
Nothing about her shrewd behind
He had not known, or guessed, before;
Goosing her in the way she loved
He loved her for the goose she was.

Belle proved a more moral story:
Princess of Parallelograms,
She favoured a straight line in bed.
Observe poor Byron with his foot
Poking a horizontal bore.

Sister and wife improved milord –
The one by liking what he did,
The other by munching apples
While he did it, even asking
'Have you finished?' when he hadn't.

Childe Byron loved and loathed them both
Yet lived with neither lady long.
Turning his back on each dark Muse,
Into the sun's doom see him limp
To die of Greece and liberty.

LATE VICTORIAN SONNET

Dead leaves his cloak, his only wand the swan
Drawing a silent circle on the lake
To conjure several old boots in its wake,
The Queen's still potent but disgraced magician,
Lord Oscar Autumn – whose last amazing trick
Turned all the usual sweets of summer sick –
Having done time for this crime of not sawing
Women in half, bursts out of gaol he-hawing
Like the bad ass he is, unbuttoning his flies . . .
Trumpets arrest him! Oscar blinks his eyes.
A pearl-pale hand beckons from a closed carriage.
Veiled lady. A proposal. It is not marriage.
Oscar is honoured, though the act's obscene,
And buggers off to Paris with the Queen.

THE SISTERS

Quick snow is falling, melting as it falls;
She stands between the fireplace and the night
Watching each soft flake flower on the pane,
Half-listening to her sister playing scales –
Their old piano's keys that click and stick –
While in the grate coals crackle together.

These things are more real to you than the scene
You know on waking, but are not a dream:
Notes rising, falling, tired music talking
About the instrument on which it plays;
A firelit room, uncurtained; two sisters
Themselves more slow to vanish than the snow.

Oh, who are they? And where is this grey house?
You have seen one sister perhaps, though not
At a winter window all mothed over.
The details of the vision fall apart;
It was your need first drew them together
Into a storm of changes and desire.

Still, do not doubt that soon enough you'll stand
Between night and the sisters, in the porch
Of the old house, hearing that piano.
And when the music stops and the door opens
Who will you say you are, and why come hither
Out of a world where snow melts as it falls?

CATCHING LEAVES

The boy you were caught leaves that fell
From trees he could not name.
The man you are must try to tell
Rowan from ash, yet run as well
To catch each falling flame
And hope upon its fame.

THE CASTLE OF THE PERFECT ONES

You'll find no mirrors in that cold abode –
Their faces are too fine for mirroring,
The perfect ones, last heirs of a long line
Who raised the dead by looking at each other
In table tops and spoons, a family
In love with its own ghosts and origins,
Homeless at home with nowhere just next door.

Pity those complete strangers their perfection.
Your funeral bores them with its brilliant doom,
Though being jealous not to let their shadows
Fall in the grave, they kneel as is seemly
And do not grin too much behind clasped hands.
They pray the resurrection, when it comes,
Will not prove irresistible to all.

You'll eat no honey in that bee-hive house
(They need no sweets who are themselves so pure)
But in your ears a buzz of holy hymns
Will sound all day, all night, immaculate,
Making the door vibrate on its cracked hinges.
What would you give to pass that door again
And see the stars from the shelving side of the hill!

The prick of perfection lengthens any note
By one exacting half . . . So will they stretch you,
Those moral musicians, to your highest pitch
And half a time beyond it. You will know
You are in royal purgatory all right,
A voice in the eternal choir that sings
From the dark tower at the back of the north wind.

Whether this is your home is not the question.
Once in the Castle of the Perfect Ones
Better to be a perfect one yourself
Than to go mad longing for imperfections.
It could be worse. At least you will be faultless
And have no need of mirrors, food, or sense –
Your selfish excellency, a perfect fool.

MNEMOSYNE

The Lady Memory disguised in moonlight
Walks the walled garden that I call my mind.
She is the mother of the other Muses;
If you approach her gently you may find
Her shadow is a nightingale, her dress
Some silken thought of long-spun tenderness.

Memory's face reminds me of her daughters
Who once were the delight of my despair.
I have forgotten much, but still remember
The way they sang their songs and combed their hair
On a green hillside where a grove of trees
Made music like a parliament of bees.

Peace to those beauties who have left me here
With my own words to eat, a bitter diet
Sweetened by drinking from the Pierian spring.
Good morrow, Memory; it is your quiet
I must learn now, not so much reticence
As knowing there is little improves silence.

ON A LEAF USED AS A BOOK-MARK

A leaf, blown back towards the pool
Against the stream's unwavering flow,
Obeys the wind's unspoken wish
To have it so.

So once was I instruction's fool
Upon the surface of delight,
Compelled to contrariety
By day, by night.

You took me in your thrifty hand,
You plucked me from the burning brook;
You dried me out and cured me
In your good book.

Now no more flotsam, I'm the mark
Which tells you how much you have read.
I who was wind–blown and alive
Lie here, not dead.